FBA Product Research 101

A First-Time FBA Seller's Guide
to Understanding Product Research Behind
Amazon's Most Profitable Products

Red Mikhail

Copyright © 2021 Red Mikhail

The moral right of this author has been asserted.

All rights reserved. No part of this publication may be reproduced, stored in a retrieval system, or transmitted in any form or by any means, without the prior permission in writing from the publisher.

The publisher is not responsible for websites (or their content) that are not owned by the publisher.

TABLE OF CONTENTS

Why This Book, Why Now? ... *page 5*

Chapter 1 - The Perfect Criteria for Beginners ... *page 10*

Chapter 2 - Let's Do Real-Life Examples ... *page 21*

Chapter 3 – Finding a Supplier ... *page 37*

Chapter 4 – Ten Things That Make Me Go Hmmm ... *page 50*

Chapter 5 - Value Skewing ... *page 60*

Chapter 6 - Practicing Your Research Muscle ... *page 76*

Conclusion ... *page 95*

BONUS CHAPTERS

For the newly updated version of this book, I added the following chapters.

Bonus Chapter #1: How the Pandemic Affects Your Product Research Process ... *page 80*

Bonus Chapter #2: Additional Notes About Private Label Potential ... *page 88*

Bonus Chapter # 3 - Profitability Calculator ... *page 94*

All in all, there are over 20+ pages of new material that will hopefully serve you and your e-commerce business. Enjoy!

Introduction: Why This Book, Why Now?

When I wrote my first book about getting started with Fulfillment by Amazon (FBA) 5 years ago, I never thought in my wildest dreams that it would be one of the best-selling titles of all time about making money on FBA for beginners.

At that time, all I wanted to do was to show new sellers how to get started with FBA step by step and without overwhelm. Today, that book has almost 1,000 reviews and around 80% of it are 4-5 stars. It still boggles my mind that one tiny eBook turned into something that thousands of people rely on to start their own Amazon based business.

So in the spirit of that book, I'm now producing a 2nd one that will hopefully have the same effect as the first.

Although I've discussed product research deeply in that first book, I realize now that a lot has changed in the industry and I cannot just give people the fish anymore. I now have to teach people how to fish.*

[With that said, that book is regularly updated with new information every 6 months].*

FOR BEGINNERS ONLY?

Like the first book, this will still be aimed for beginners or first-time sellers. So if you're someone who already has at least 5 years of experience as a seller, then this is probably not for you – or you can just skip to chapter 4 and beyond as those chapters will focus more on the mindset and strategies behind Amazon's most profitable products.

***

Let me give you a brief overview of the process.

The book is divided into 6 chapters:

1 - The Perfect Criteria for Beginners

Chapter 1 focuses on the criteria that I recommend beginners to follow. A product can be profitable yet it can still be unsuitable for beginners. There's a lot of factors that may affect your choice of product to sell and being a complete beginner make things very different for you.

2 - Let's Do Real-Life Examples

In this part, I'll show you some real-life examples of products to sell as a beginner and I'll explain my thinking behind it. The point is not for you to choose my examples. The point is to show you the rationale behind my choices.

3 – Finding a Supplier

This part focuses on finding a supplier for your product. Should you import from China? Should you produce it locally? How do you know what to do? This chapter explains all that stuff.

4 – 10 Things That Make Me Go Hmmm…

When you've been selling for quite a while, you get to learn the greatest factors that affects your sales. Think of this chapter as the best-practices to follow when you're researching a product.

5 - Value Skewing

Whether you're a beginner or an advance seller, this is going to be the defining chapter of this book. Why? Because it focuses on a timeless skill that will serve you for the rest of your career. I know that that seems like a big claim. But this simple concept will give you so much leverage and advantage that you'll want to give me a thousand bucks after you read it.

6 - Practicing Your Research Muscle

Chapter 6 is about practice. It's about building your research skills so you'll get better at it and eventually find more profitable products. It's a skill that all serious seller should have – whether they're a beginner, intermediate seller, or advance.

Combining all of these concepts will make you a product idea machine. This means you're going to look at products in the eyes of an expert whose focus is not just product research but also value creation.

After reading this book, you'll be able to see something special in items that most sellers just completely ignore.

So go grab a coffee, sit back, relax and let's get started.

Chapter 1 - The Perfect Criteria for Beginners

There's something that you have to know about me. I don't always follow the criteria that I'm going to teach you.

Why?

Because I'm not a beginner anymore. I've been in this business for quite some time now and my criteria for a perfect product differs from that of a new seller.

However, I do recommend that you follow what I'll teach you because this is the criteria that – in my obviously biased opinion – has the best chance of helping you succeed as a new seller.

Here's another thing to take note of. You don't have to follow the criteria to the teeth. Just because one criterion is missing doesn't mean that the product you chose sucks. Think of these as guideposts instead of rules.

Sure, you can follow the rules and stick to it – that will serve you a lot. But you shouldn't be limited by them. Let it guide you but never let it define what you do.

THE CRITERIA:

#1 – Price of $20-$100 on Amazon

As a beginner, your focus is on selling as much of your products as possible. This way, you'll know what works and what doesn't.

Imagine trying to sell a $450 product. Sure, you'll probably make more money with a more expensive product but you won't really get any activity every day. (Thus, you don't have any data to study).

For most consumer, a product priced at more than $100 requires a lot of thinking and deliberation. Also, at that price point, customers tend to be more brand-focused.

For example, you won't buy a smartwatch from a random company. Your choices are probably Apple Vs. Samsung, and then the other smaller smartwatch producers (that relatively speaking, still has a pretty big brand).

In this case, selling a private labeled $150 smartwatch won't work.

This is why I recommend selling products within the $20-$100 price point. The price is high enough that it's still possible to make $30-$50 net profit per sale but it's also low enough that most people can still afford it.

A product that requires less deliberation – something that you'll buy in a snap – is better for beginners, generally speaking.

FBA products tend to give an average of 30%-40% net profit after all the product expenses and fees. So a $30 product will likely give you a $10-$15 net profit. Sell 5 of that every day and you now have a part-time income of $1500 per month.

#2 – The 5x Rule

This rule states that you shouldn't sell anything that you can't import or produce for 5x less its Amazon (or market) price.

In simple terms, if a product on Amazon sells for $50, you should be able to import or produce that for only $10 per piece.

But why?

It's because we want to make money. I know, hardly a novel concept.

When it comes to selling on Amazon, there are fees that you need to pay. In general, those fees will hover around 35% of the total price on average.
So if a product on Amazon sells for $50, then you can safely assume that $17.5 will go to the fees. If you produce it for $10 apiece, then your total expense will be: $27.5

$50-$27.5 = $22.5 is your net profit.

If you pay for advertisements, then that will add up as well. Plus, remember, shipping fee (from production to Amazon warehouse) may also add up to the price. In reality, your total net profit, in this case, would be at around $15 - $18.

So to be on the safe side, you should only choose products you can sell for at least 5x its production cost. By following this criteria, you can safely assume that you'll be getting at least 20% net profit. Which is actually pretty good – especially if you're doing a lot volume-wise.

#3 – Light, Relatively Small and Easy to Ship

Let's face it, big and heavy products are hard and expensive to ship. If you chose a big and heavy product, then your cost of doing business becomes too high that it'll be almost impossible to earn a decent profit.

Unless you already have experience when it comes to that specific product or category, I recommend going for the light and small product path.
What is light and what is small in this case?

My take on this is if it's something that you can put on your small backpack without it being bothersome, then it is light and small.

#4 – High-Potential for Private Labelling as a Beginner

I would assume that you're in this business for the long-term. You want to create a brand and you want to sell stuff over and over again.

In that case, you need to choose a product with a higher potential of being private-labeled.

You can't really private label a phone can you? It'll be too expensive and it will cost you millions (or billions) to compete with other brands like Apple, Samsung, Huawei, etc.

You have to find a product that you can sell even without having a mega-brand.

You can't compete with Apple's MacBook. But you definitely can compete with OXO's Dish Brush. You can improve it, get better materials, change the handle grip, change colors, etc. Doing those things won't cost you billions.

Remember, private labelling is when you hire someone to produce the product for you and then put your own brand in it. Make sure that the product you chose is worthy of being private-labeled.

This doesn't mean that you can't compete with name brands. There are still hundreds if not thousands of sub-categories out there that aren't dominated by name brands. But you should know what battles to fight in and what battles to ignore for now.

Note: If you want a more detailed explanation of this concept, go skip to the bonus chapter

#2 and come back here once you finished reading that part.

#5 – Evergreen

I'm not really a fan of selling seasonal products. I like making money whether it's Christmas or it's summertime. Sure, products will always have their peak months but I also want some sense of evergreen'ess if that makes sense?

I want something that will sell day-in and day-out. Something that people use regularly.

For example, a dishwasher brush is something that most households have. It's not just something that you buy for Christmas or Halloween.
This is what I mean by choosing an evergreen product. I want to make money whatever the season it may be.

#6 – Room for Improvement

This is the most important criteria. I want a product that I can improve upon.

The good news is every product out there can still be improved. To improve a product, you have to have the mindset of a producer. Someone who sees problems as opportunities.

For example, a dish brush can be improved through:

a – Adding an electric component so you can make it automatic. Sort of like an electric toothbrush for the dishes.

b – You can change the handle grip for a more stickier one.

c – You can add colors so people have more choices

The point is improving a product requires that you put yourself in the position of the consumer. You have to find what they hate and what they love about the product.

***

A Category to Avoid for Now

If you are a complete beginner, I would recommend that you avoid the following category:

Anything related to consumer electronics. Stuff like smartphones, flash drives, dongles, etc.

They're just too competitive and a lot of messy stuff happens behind the scene that's hardly worth making an extra few hundred bucks for. Imagine shipping 2,000 flash drives on Amazon only to find out that 50% of them are ineffective. Dios Mio!

The horror that will ensue from that carnage will break – pardon my words – the f out of you. Avoid them until you have more experience and capital.

In the next chapter, I'll give you some examples of products that I think are good for beginners and I'll explain my rationale behind them. This will be a good exercise for your mind because you're sort of getting a behind the scenes of what happens before a product gets chosen.

Chapter 2 - Let's Do Real-Life Examples

I can explain things all day long or I can show you how to choose a product instead.

In this chapter, I'm going to give you a deep dive into how I do research for new products to sell on Amazon FBA.

It all starts with the category.

Quite honestly, the category doesn't really matter that much. Just avoid electronics and choose anything on Amazon's best-seller department here:

https://www.amazon.com/Best-Sellers/zgbs/

Choose anything you're interested in. The product matters more than the category.

Also, quick tip: Choose a sub-category under a larger category. So don't just find products in the "Kitchen & Dining" department. Go deeper and look for sub-categories under it.

Kitchen & Dining
- Bar Tools & Drinkware
- Coffee, Tea & Espresso Appliances
- Kitchen & Table Linens
- Small Appliances
- Wine Accessories
- Bakeware
- Cookware
- Home Brewing & Wine Making
- Cutlery & Knife Accessories
- Kitchen Utensils & Gadgets
- Storage & Organization
- Glassware & Drinkware
- Dining & Entertaining

Alright, let's do an example.

EXAMPLE #1 – Dish Brush

Under Kitchen & Dining, I found this OXO Good Grips Brush.

I used this one as an example in chapter 1 so we might as well continue with it.

Basically, this is a product that cleans your dishes. That's it.

Let's run it down in our criteria:

#1 – Price of $20-$100 on Amazon

This one sells for $20 and it's for a set. I found others that sell for $14 and some for $16. The point is it hovers around the $15-20 area.

This one passes this criteria of having a product that sells for $20 [or very close to it].

#2 – The 5x Rule

To know how much the product can be produced for, I usually go to ALIBABA.COM and search for a product similar to it.

While doing my research, I found that the price ranges from $1.5 per piece to $2 per piece.

Not bad. Remember, this may still increase depending on the number of orders and if you'll add some features that will make the product more expensive to produce.

#3 – Light, Relatively Small and Easy to Ship

This one is obviously light and small. It's a brush, not a damn stove.

So this will be quite easy and inexpensive to ship.

#4 – High-Potential for Private Labelling as a Beginner

I would say YES to this because there are no name-brands already dominating this category. It's not like a consumer product with a loyal following. It's not something that people share on their wall or talk about with their friends.

If they can find a better alternative to what they already have (or if they found my version better looking, more useful, easier to use or much more effective according to the Amazon reviews) then they will buy it.

#5 – Evergreen

You need a dish brush whether it's summer or winter. You need a dish brush whether you're living in New York or Los Angeles. This product isn't ethnicity or race-specific as well

(I mean, duh – but this is a big issue nowadays so I feel like I have to mention it even though it absolutely has nothing to do with the product). Okay, I'm going off the tangent here, where are we again?

Oh right, it's about choosing an evergreen product. Something that you tend to use regularly. In this case, it's every day. If you don't wash your dishes every day then that's just disgusting behavior. Yayks!

#6 – Room for Improvement

There's definitely room for improvement. I can use a different material for the brush. Change the colors to more premium colors like rose gold or matte back. I can add some electronic things on it to make it automatic.

Overall Rating: A B C or D

For my overall rating, I would give this one a B. I would've given this an overall rating of A if it wasn't for the last criteria. Yes, it can be improved upon, but it'll just be minor things like colors and some material resources. Still, those minor things do add up. It's a solid B and it's something I would've considered highly back when I was just a beginner.

EXAMPLE #2 – Collapsible Car Trunk Organizer by FORTEM

#1 – Price of $20-$100 on Amazon

This one ranges from $25 up to $100 at the high-end spectrum. It's not the cheapest thing in the world but it's also not expensive. I would say it's in the goldilocks zone when it comes to the price. I'd give this a solid A from the price perspective.

#2 – The 5x Rule

Depending on the quality of your design and product, the cost may vary from $5-$20 per piece.

This may seem cheap but this can get expensive especially if there's a minimum order quantity of 100 pieces or more.

Still, this is a good product for a beginner. Not too expensive but not too cheap either. It's just right.

#3 – Light, Relatively Small and Easy to Ship

This one looks huge and heavy. But it's actually not.

This can be folded [a major thing when it comes to shipping] and the weight isn't that heavy. It's around 1 kg. to 3 kg. per piece. The less designed versions are lighter, cheaper and easier to ship as well – so you can get started with that version.

#4 – High-Potential for Private Labelling as a Beginner

Yes. You can still compete in this category and there's a lot of new things that you can do to make this a worthy project. Plus, the price point isn't too expensive either (around $3-$20 per piece).

#5 – Evergreen

There are millions of car owners and there's always a constant need for a trunk organizer that works well.

Look at your car. There are probably dozens of items in there that's just inside the car but you barely even use. You say that you'll use them "just in case" but they're already cluttering up your car.

Plus, you can also use it when you need to put something in your car and you don't want it to just be bouncing around while you drive.

See? Everyone needs this product even if they don't know they need it.

#6 – Room for Improvement

Right out of the bat, the first thing I noticed about this product is the potential for improvement or change.

If you can produce some added value for the customers (even as simple as a handle for when they take it off the car) can be a big deal for the customers.

You can also add different colors, change the materials and find something that will make it better for them. We will discuss this more in chapters 4 and 5.

Overall Rating: A B C or D

I would personally give this product an A as it matches the criteria well. The perfect product doesn't exist but this one's a pretty good way to get started.

(Obviously, don't just take my word for it. Make sure that you understand the mindset behind choosing the product and not just the specific product itself).

*

Alright, let's do one more example.

EXAMPLE #3 – Ankle Stabilizer

#1 – Price of $20-$100 on Amazon

This one is at around the $20-$25 mark on Amazon. So this passes our price criteria.

#2 – The 5x Rule

Looking at similar products on Alibaba, I found that most ankle stabilizers cost $3-$5 per piece.

So this one fits our 5x rule.

#3 – Light, Relatively Small and Easy to Ship

At only 6.4 ounces with a product dimension of 8.2 x 5.2 x 2.3 inches, it's super light and very small at the same time.

I'll give it an A in this department.

Product Dimensions: 8.2 x 5.2 x 2.3 inches ; 5.6 ounces
Shipping Weight: 6.4 ounces (View shipping rates and policies)

#4 – High-Potential for Private Labelling as a Beginner

A definite yes. This is the type of product that most beginners can get started with. It's light, it's cheap and it's something you can easily add a brand on without adding too much expensive stuff to improve the product.

#5 – Evergreen

This is the part where it misses the mark a little. It's just isn't something you use daily unless you're really into sports or you have some injury.

Still, a lot of people do use the product and it's a niche product that has lots of potential.

#6 – Room for Improvement

There is definitely a lot of room for improvement.

Just reading at the reviews, the first improvement I thought of was the sizing guide. This has nothing to do with the product itself but more on the marketing side. If you can help the buyers easily find the right fit for them – then making an order on your listing will be a no-brainer.

I see a lot of complaints in the reviews and they are mostly about having the wrong size and fit. I'll teach you more about this on the chapter of value skewing but hopefully, you're having a small epiphany about product research as you read this.

It's not just about the product, it's also about the marketing and the after service you provide.

With that said, I can also see that adding some kind of new material, adding sizes or changing the design can help you add more value to the customers.

Overall Rating: A B C or D

I can't really decide whether it's an A or B so I'll give this one an A- instead. The reason I can't give it a solid A is because of the evergreen factor. I don't really see it as a "need" – more like something you use for sports, injury or when you specifically need ankle support. Still, it's a good product and it's something that a lot of people use.

***

Now that you have a pretty solid idea of how to use the criteria for product research, the next step is to find a supplier who can help you produce and private label the product for you.

Chapter 3 – Finding a Supplier

Finding the perfect supplier is like kissing a lot of frogs hoping that you'll eventually find the prince charming. Except, in this case, it's 1,000 times harder.

Why? Because the perfect supplier doesn't exist. Brad Pitt doesn't exist in this e-commerce universe.

So what should you do then? Well, just like everybody else in this business, you just kiss a lot of frogs – because the good news is a lot of them turn to Matt Damon anyway as long as you know where to find them.

Now let me show you how to find your Matt Damon.

1 – Google

The easiest way to get started is to search for keywords related to your product.

Here are some based keywords to search for when looking for a supplier:

Product + supplier

Product + country + suppliers

Product + private label

Product + made from

Supplier of + product

Supplier of product + specific country

For example...

If I'm searching for a dish brush supplier, I can do these searches:

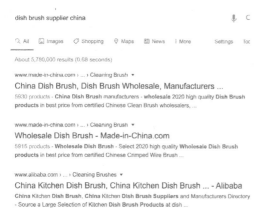

dish brush supplier china

supplier of dish brush

2 – TTNET.NET

Another one of the resources I love is TTNET.

It's very straightforward to use and there's a lot of manufacturers here that offer a better deal compared to Alibaba.

Just search for the product you are looking for and you'll get hundreds of potential suppliers.

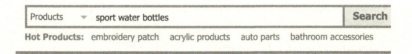

You can also search by category and even use this as a product research tool. Remember, the product you chose in the beginning doesn't have to be your final product. You can still do some research and find something better.

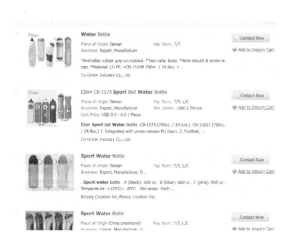

Also, important tip: whenever you're searching for a product and talking to a company here, make sure that you're talking to a MANUFACTURER and NOT A WHOLESALER. Wholesalers will make the product 20% more expensive for you. Yes, they will accept smaller orders which are good as samples but avoid dealing with wholesalers as much as possible.

Take Note: It should say "Manufacturer" in the sales method. You'll see it below the product category.

Product Category:	Sport Water Bottles, Promotional Sports Gear, Bicycle Water Bottles
Sales Method:	Export, Manufacture
Payment Term:	T/T, L/C

Also, click on their company name to find out more about them.

Make sure that you read up details about their business before you hire them or before you even inquire about them.

42

3 – HKTDC

If you can't find suppliers on TTNET.NET, then you have another resource to use which is HKTDC.

This one is actually much bigger and you'll find more suppliers producing more types of products.

When you do your research, make sure that you tick on the MANUFACTURER only checkbox.

You may also want to consider the "credentials" bar and check out their certificates and verifications. Not all companies will have these credentials, but the more of these they have, the better that company probably is.

Again, don't forget to read up more details about the company.

4 – ALIBABA

This is pretty common and most people go here first. The process is pretty much the same – you go search for your product and then look at different suppliers.

Here are the most important things to remember when you're using ALIBABA to source your products.

1 - Make sure that the suppliers have complete trade assurance. You will find this info in their product listing.

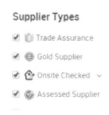

2 – Choose a supplier that has more than 5 years of experience. This information is also available in their Alibaba company profile.

3 - The response rate should be higher than 60%. The higher and more responsive they are, the better. This means faster back & forth communication. Be mindful of their office hours though. For Chinese manufacturers, their office hours are between 8am-6pm Beijing. That's 7pm to 5am EST.

4 – The devil is in the details.

Try to learn more about their company and find as much information about them.

You can also make a quick Google search about their business and make sure that they don't have any pending cases or scam complaints.

Local Vs. International

So when does it make sense to source locally or internationally?

Well it all comes down to 3 things:

1 – Finance

Financially speaking, does it make sense to source something for $5 each when you can get it in China for $1? From this perspective, it makes more sense to get it from China – because it's 5x more expensive if you source it locally.

However, I haven't told you the product price yet. What if something "Made in the U.S.A." can sell for 5x more as well? Are your potential customers paying that much on Amazon? Or it makes much more sense to get it from China since the market isn't ready yet to pay a premium for having it made in America?

Do your research. Go to Amazon.com and search for your most expensive competitor. Then do the numbers. Can you produce it in America [or wherever you are locally] and sell it for a more premium price? If yes, then you know what to do.

2 – Quality

There's a stereotype that things that are *Made in China* are far less superior than something that is made in the U.S.A. – although this has been true in the past, I don't believe that this is the case anymore.
The iPhone you're using is made in China. Clearly, those guys know what they're doing.

So you just have to find suppliers that are proven to create quality products. It's not about the country anymore. It's about that specific product and the supplier's ability to create a high-quality product.

3 – Market Expectation

There are just certain products that amass a following just by being source nationally or locally. There's a certain appeal about something being created in your own country. Sometimes, it's not even about the product itself. It's about the business. People like supporting their own. They feel good about being part of a community that helps someone that has the same identity as them – in this case, it's the nationality – *American Made baby!*

Although quite truthfully, this factor matters much less if you're selling a product via Amazon.com. However, if you're selling through your own e-commerce brand website, then Made in whatever country matters more.

Chapter 4 – Ten Things That Make Me Go Hmmm

These are my best tips when it comes to doing your product research. Now, this is extremely personal and it's not something that everyone should follow. Just like the criteria I gave earlier, you should use this as a guidepost and not as a rule of law (except for #9 and #10 – those 2 are a MUST-FOLLOW for any serious FBA seller).

#1 – Anti-Fragile

Personally, I'm not a fan of selling items that easily breaks. Stuff like mugs, plates, or anything that is made from easily breakable glass.

Can you make money selling these types of items?

For sure. A lot of it actually.

But the hassle and headache you'll encounter trying to ship these types of products just isn't worth it, especially if you're a beginner.

The undeniable fact is fragile items are just a pain in the butt to ship. Plus, since they are made of glasses or easily breakable material – they tend to be heavier which then adds up to the cost of shipping.

And if they break along the way, then you are f**ked. Sure, there are insurance and all that stuff, but that's another thing to deal with.

Unless you already have lots of experience and capital, I suggest you stay away from fragile items.

#2 – Non-Brand Dominated

This means not competing with companies that are already in the "culture" of that product.

What do I mean by that?

Let's say that you want to sell a China-made phone. Well, you have to compete with Apple, Samsung, Huawei, and other multi-billion dollar companies. There's just no way you can compete in that product category.

Now, these all still depends on the product. In our example in the last chapter, we talk about the dish brush. There are a lot of multi-million dollar companies selling a brush like that. But if you think about it, that type of product isn't really ingrained in our modern culture. Nobody talks about a dish brush to their friends or family – still, the product is an obvious need and something that every household should have.

#3 – Seasonal (But Only If)

As I showed you in the criteria, I prefer to sell products that are evergreen. Something that would sell whatever the season – January to December.

So this will come as a personal preference. Let's say that you only want to become a part-time seller and you only want to do it from November to January (where sales are 3x-5x higher than normal months).

In this case, you can find a product that is related to Halloween, Christmas, and New Year.

Another example is if you only want to sell during the winter months. If this is the case, then you can focus on winter-related products and you should expect your sales to be high during winter months and low during summer.

The choice is totally up to you. The good news is this business is quite flexible and you have your choice of work hours and the effort you want to put in.

#4 – Lightweight

The reason why I prefer lightweight products is because of the shipping cost. On average, the shipping will be at around 20%-30% of the total cost of the product. Sometimes, even more.

A lightweight product – especially if it's small, will always be cheaper to ship. For most beginners without huge capital, saving money on shipping is a big deal as it can make or break their profits.

#5 – Keep Following the 5X Rule

The 5X rule states that the price of the product you sell on Amazon should be at least 5x the amount you originally pay per piece for the product.

If a product sells on Amazon for $100, then the original cost per piece from the supplier shouldn't be more than $20. Remember, you still have to pay for shipping to Amazon warehouses, Amazon fees and other fees like product inspection.

I recommend following this rule as it'll give you a safe margin of error and it'll help you get to breakeven, and eventually the positive ROI.

#6 - Ability to Expand + Long-Term Thinking

If you're here for the long-term then you have to find a product that you can build something on. If you chose to sell barbecue gloves, then you have to find other products that are related to that as well. Stuff like grills, tongs, heck – maybe even your own barbecue sauce in the future.

Don't just choose random products. Think about the future as well. Is this something you can build upon? Would you be willing to work on this type of item in the foreseeable future?

The answer must be yes.

#7 – Recurring Purchases

If you can find a product that you can sell for more than $20 every month and a lot of your customers purchase month after month, then you'll be set forever.

This type of product requires deep research. In general, recurring purchases happen on products that are cheaper than $20. This makes sense since the consumers have limited spending budget and most people don't have $100 to spend on any recurring (monthly, weekly) purchases.

#8 – Boring Products Make Money

Here's something that most newbie sellers forget.

The marketmind doesn't care about your passion or what you like. Just because you think a product is boring doesn't mean you shouldn't consider selling it.
In fact, most successful FBA sellers I know sell surprisingly boring products. Stuff that we use every day and barely even think about. Those are my favorite types of products as well.

I don't care if the product doesn't make me feel all happy and giddy inside. If the market needs it, then I'll sell it.

#9 – Find a Hole and Fill It

Of all the things that we talk about in this chapter, this and the next one are the most important to follow.

This is how you win in the AMAZON FBA game.

You focus on finding an under-served market. Products that most sellers already forget about because there's a new shiny thing that most people are into at the moment.

The first step is to find that hole and know exactly what's wrong and what's missing.

After that, you create a solution that solves the market's issues and problems.

That's how you win. Simple as that.

(We'll discuss this one in detail on the next chapter)

#10 – Focus on Value Creation, Not Competition

I never get most gurus obsession with the competition.

"Oh you have to do this keyword research, then analyze every single competition, then you gotta run this software, then this other software…"

Although pre-research and knowing the numbers are very important, nothing beats the research of someone whose focus is on value creation.

After finding the hole, you have to create the best solution for that problem.
If you focus on value, then all you have to do is trust the market and hope that it accepts what you can offer.

The market will always decide whether who wins or who loses.

I know. Hope really isn't a strategy. But you need to focus on what you can control (problem-solving and value creation) and just let go of what you can't (what the competition does and what the market does).

Ultimately, especially in the long-term. The ones who win are those who are hell-bent in solving other people's problems.

Chapter 5 - Value Skewing

In this chapter, I'm going to introduce you to a concept that changed my life – and hopefully yours as well.

In simple terms, value skewing is about finding something that you can improve on a currently existing product. This also applies to services and pretty much other entrepreneurial ventures. But for the sake of our discussion, we're going to focus on products available on Amazon.com.

What I'll do is explain the strategy behind it and then we'll do an example on how to actually do it in the real world.

When it comes to value skewing, there are 2 main questions you should be asking yourself:

A – What's wrong with the product?

What are the things that are missing? What features and benefits are the customers looking for?

B – How can I improve it?

What are the things that you can do to add value?

THE PROCESS

Here's my usual process for skewing value out of current products on Amazon.

#1 – Search on Amazon.com

Search for your type of product on Amazon. This is literally just typing your product name and then looking at different products available on Amazon.com

Choose 5 products similar to what you want to make and copy & paste their listing links to a new word file.

I recommend naming the file: Product Name + Value Skew [crossfitgripsvalueskew.docx].

#2 – Look at the Negative Reviews [1 to 3 stars]

Read ALL the negative reviews and try to understand what's missing from the product. What are the things that they are complaining about? What are the problems that the current iteration of this product doesn't solve?

Copy & paste those reviews on your research word file as well. (Do the same on the following as well)

#3 – Look at the Positive Reviews [4 to 5 stars]

Most of the time, there will be more positive reviews than negative ones. When you're reading the positive ones, remember that you're looking for the common denominator. What are the things that they like about the product? Usually, there will be 2-3 features/benefits that will appear over and over again. Beside the rating, you will see the keywords that appear over and over again in the reviews. You will find these keywords on the top of the review section. These are the clues that will lead you to what they like and what they don't like about the product.

Read reviews that mention

push button   good grips   rubber button   soap dispenser
highly recommend   storage set   pots and pans   dispensing button
scrub brush   dish soap   long time   grips dish   catches the water

#4 – Scour the Forums & Talk to Your Potential Customers

The next step is to learn more about your market by reading forums related to your product.

Think of this as another form of market research.

I recommend searching for the following terms on Google:

Product name + reviews

Product name + forums

Product name + Reddit

Product name + Quora

Product name + Yahoo answers

Best + Product Name

For example, you can do searches like:

"Collapsible car trunk reviews"

"Collapsible car trunk reddit"

"Collapsible car trunk forum"

Or

"Best Collapsible car trunk"

"Collapsible car trunk yahoo answers"

"Collapsible car trunk Quora"

Your aim is to find out more about the market. What are the things they are complaining about? What are the things that you can change in response to their complaints?

Another thing that you can do is to talk to your potential customers. Ask them what works best for them and what products are they currently using to solve their current problems regarding that topic.

Sure, this takes more work and requires more effort. But you're trying to get ahead of the market and taking your time to do this gives you a lot of advantage.

When you sell your product, you want the market to think: "Wow, this seller just gets me."

#5 – Discover New and/or Underserved Markets

As you read more about your customers' issues, sometimes you'll inevitably come up with new markets or underserved markets to target. For example, as you research about your product about CrossFit tape you may find that a new type of market needs one as well [Instead of normal crossfit fans, maybe you can target body builders, runners, basketball players, football players, etc.].

You'll never know when these new markets will arise. So make sure to keep your mind open and actively look for new opportunities as you do your product research.

#6 – Come Up with a Solution

After your research, you will find some common problems that the current marketplace is not solving yet.

Now it's time to consolidate your research and come up with possible solutions to the market's problem. It could be as simple as changing the handle grip of your brush, adding [or subtracting] an ingredient to your protein powder. What you'll do will depend on what the market is looking for. There's no one size fits all solution here.

It's up to you as the entrepreneur to find out what changes need to be done. You are the seller, it's your job to come up with the best solution you can provide.

Real-World Amazon Value Skewing

Example – Gymnastics Grip

#1 – Search on Amazon.com

Find at least 5 products that are similar to what you want to produce. In our example, I will choose *Bar Grips*.

#2 – Look at the Negative Reviews

Next, copy-paste the negative reviews after you read them. Make sure that you try to understand what's wrong with the product and what you can do about it.

In this case, I found that the issues are mostly about:

1 – The dye in the product doesn't last long because of sweat.

2 – The strap cuts into the wrists.

3 – It breaks fast (usually within 2-4 weeks).

#3 – Look at the Positive Reviews

The next step is to read positive reviews.

Find out the best features or qualities of these products and make sure that you're going to incorporate them into your own version.

[Read the negative and positive reviews of about 5 different products before you move on to the next step]

TIP: Also read the Q & A's available in the listing as these are usually the customers' common concerns before they buy the product.

#4 – Scour the Forums & Talk to Your Potential Customers

The next step is to search for your product on forums and other sites like Reddit, Quora and Yahoo Answers.

You will also find problems occurring here that you should add to the list of "issues" about that product.

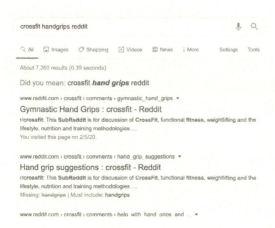

> **bighomie105** 1 point · 3 years ago
> I have tried a lot of them as well. My biggest issue with the leather grips is that they are too thick and I don't feel like I can grip the bar. I personally like the Natural Grip. I don't have to fidget with them during the WOD by taking them off for barbell movements. I just leave them on. They don't mess with my grip which is why I like them so much.
>
> **[deleted]** 1 point · 3 years ago
> JAW grips worked really well for me.
>
> **PM_ME_UR_YOGA_BOOTY** if I lift this can I eat that? 1 point · 3 years ago
> I just got a pair of Rogue V2's and haven't used gymnastic grips before, so take that into account.
> I like the V2's. I've used them 4-5 times, I don't find them too thick but they offer good protection. Apparently there is a break in period with grips but mine seem good to go from the start.
>
> **arq68** 1 point · 3 years ago
> I've tried a few different brands and settled on these as the best ones for me

In this example above, the problem is the leather is too thick which makes gripping the bar harder. That's a problem you can possibly solve! That's basically value skewing in a nutshell. Find a problem, then come up with a possible solution.

#5 – Discover New and/or Underserved Markets

In this case, I found that a gymnastics grip has a lot of uses. It can be for gymnastics, CrossFit, lifting and other workouts that require you to use your hand in gripping something.

This means I have a lot of options on what market to choose. I can choose to specialize in CrossFit and create a version that's exactly for those types of users. Even though this will make my market size smaller, it'll help me rise over other grips since mine is especially tailor-made for the CrossFit market.

#6 – Come Up with a Solution

Through my research about gymnastic grips, the common problems that I saw are the following:

1 – It breaks easily. This is the number one issue.

2 – The dye comes off in 2-4 weeks and it sticks to the hand because of sweat.

3 – The material is not grippy enough.

4 – Size issues.

THE SOLUTION:

1 – It breaks easily. This is the number one issue.

Talk to my supplier about using a different type of material that they will use to produce the product. Then produce different versions and test them out to find the best one.

2 – The dye comes off in 2-4 weeks and it sticks to the hand because of sweat.

Either avoid different colors or use a different type of dye that doesn't come off with sweat.

3 – The material is not grippy enough.

The same as the first one. Try out different materials and find the grippiest one to use.

4 – Size issues.

Do proper marketing and make sure that the size fits well for a specific customer. I saw a lot of reviews about wrong sizes and I'm thinking that this is mostly due to ineffective marketing. To solve this problem, create a size chart and post it in the listing.

*

Take note of this: Even just 1 or 2 changes from the product - as long as it's something the customers value – can completely change the way they look at your offer. Those 1 or 2 changes can be the difference between selling 20 pieces per day or 2 pieces per month. Sometimes, even just a change of listing pictures will double your sales.

Take this advice seriously and invest in pre-research and always have the mindset of a value skewer.

Value skewing is a simple concept, but powerful nonetheless. It's something that all entrepreneurs should do instead of trying to guess what the market want and needs.

In fact, I would say that it's the secret behind the most profitable Amazon products. It all comes down to solving problems that currently exist in the market. That's all there is to it.

Once you understand the strategy behind value skewing, the next step is to create a research habit so you'll never run out of great product ideas and you can improve as an Amazon FBA seller.

Chapter 6 - Practicing Your Research Muscle

Your product research skill will not be perfect especially in the beginning. You'll miss some stuff that experienced sellers will immediately notice. You'll let some good opportunities go. You'll mess up communicating with suppliers – and all shitty things will happen.

Honestly, that's to be expected from someone who's really trying…. Someone willing to go through – at times – the painful process. And I hope you're that kind of person.

Trust me, it's all going to be worth it.

Just one product can change your life.

So I recommend that you start building your product research muscle as early as now.

This means regularly following the product research and value skewing process that I laid out in this book.

Here's what I recommend that you do:

Create a Schedule

The best way to build a habit is to create a schedule for it. I suggest that you cycle through the whole process at least 2 times per week. That means searching for categories, browsing products, reading reviews, going through forums and finding solutions to the problems.

You can do it during your free time after work or during weekends.

Personally, I follow this schedule:

Wednesday – 6pm-9pm

Saturday – 9am-12nn

This allows me to find at least 2-3 solid products every week which then leads to a higher chance of picking something that will lead to a positive return on my investment (ROI).

MINDSET SHIFT

The biggest takeaway that I want you to get from this book is this.

Start looking at problems as if they are opportunities in disguise. Start actively seeking them and be aware of the possible opportunities around you.

You'll always hear people complain about their problems.

"This sucks"
"I hope there's a _____"
"Why does this x suck?"
"Why can't there be _____ [solution to this problem]

Start hearing these complaints as business opportunities.

This mindset will serve you well in your entrepreneurial journey.

Bonus Chapter #1: How the Pandemic Affects Your Product Research Process

When the pandemic started, I immediately got dozens of messages from my FBA selling friends and partners worried about how we're going to survive it, economically speaking.

They started asking what products will sell and what products won't. They started panicking and they started lowering their orders for their products.

Which is funny because I did the opposite.

Here's the truth. It doesn't change anything that much. My research process is still the same process that I laid out in this book.

It's more effective now than before! Why? Because the process that I taught you focuses on the fundamentals.

They're not about some tricks or magic research process. It's solely about choosing a good product and trying to improve it even more for the sake of the customers.

So here are my top 4 advice that can help you navigate uncertain times as we have now.

#1 - Look at the Current Trend

It's always a good idea to look at the current trend so you can have a good feel of the market.

I recommend that you start with Google Trends.

By now, you already have an idea of what type of product you want to sell. Just go to Google Trends and then type some keywords related to your product.

It's as simple as looking at the graph and making sure that those keywords are either stable or going up in searches.

I recommend a time-span of 12 months.

Also, try to look at the patterns for the last 5 years. Some products are seasonal so you should expect fewer sales in some months if you chose that type of product.

An example is a product like *a hunting bow*.

The graph below shows that the searches are generally lower from December to May and it wildly picks up from June to August.

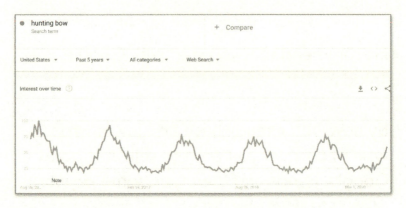

It shows the up and down depending on the season but the general trajectory of the market is consistent. This is a type of product that you know will continue to sell in the coming years. It's not just a one-off trend like fidget spinners.

Another example I can give you is the search term "fitness equipment"

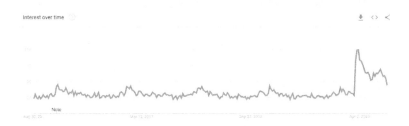

The graph above shows a massive uptick when the lockdown started last April 2020. It has now come back down but the searches are still 100% higher than the normal average searches compared to the last 5 years. This clearly shows that this category is here to stay as more and more people are now buying their own fitness equipment that they can use at home.

#2 - If the Numbers Make Sense, Go Local

The impact of the pandemic on manufacturing cannot be underestimated. It's now a little bit harder to get your product manufactured and delivered from one country to the U.S.

What you can do is be open to the idea of manufacturing your product locally (in America or your own state). I am 100% sure that this will be more expensive. However, don't just think about the profit margins. Think of this as another advantage for your brand. The U.S. made products are generally more favored than China-made ones.

If the numbers make sense and you're still making an acceptable profit, then going local might be the way to go.

Another factor to consider is the reputation of the country you're sourcing to as it relates to the product you are trying to produce.

Some countries have a better reputation based on a specific product.
For example, the Philippines and Mexico are a pretty good option for leather goods. While China is better for plastic made products.

#3 - Create a Brand Based on Quality

Now more than ever, it's important to focus on the quality of your product. In the past, you can just put random cheap products on Amazon and you'll automatically get sales. But as more and more people start their own e-commerce business, the harder it gets to make money.

Ironically, the fastest way to make money on Amazon is by simply taking it slow.

Make sure that you add features that the customers need, use high-quality materials, hire a manufacturer with a good reputation, sell your stuff well, and keep improving your products based on customer feedback.

Do these things deliberately and you'll have a better chance at success.

The secret to making money on Amazon is simple:

Create a damn good product that does what it promised to do.

#4 - Focus on the Long-Term

In the following months or years to come, an awful lot of people will be trying to start their own FBA business. The majority of them will fail because they're only doing it for the quick buck.
They don't care about producing quality products that add value to the customers. They only care about making money.

My plead to you is I hope that you focus on the long-term. The future of e-commerce is bright and those who are willing to do it the right way will make millions in the process. Don't be afraid to lose a little bit of money in the beginning. Remember, you are running a business, not a hobby. Think of your initial capital as an investment in your future.
There's no guarantee that your first product will sell but I can guarantee you that you will learn a lot from your first product.

You will learn how to deal with manufacturers, you will learn how to do the shipping, you will learn how to sell your product, you will learn how to create a better listing, and most importantly, you will learn that no amount of research and preparation can ever replace real-life experience.

Always look at the bigger picture. Focus on the long-term.

Bonus Chapter #2: Additional Notes About Private Label Potential

As I read the review of the first iteration of this book, I found that some people are a little confused when it comes to finding high potential for private label products.

So in this chapter, I want to clarify my thoughts and add some notes so you can pick the best product possible for your FBA business.

Ok, so let's define what private label is first.

Private Label is a product that you outsource/manufactured by other companies and be branded as your own.
This isn't a shady word or a shady practice. That's just how this business works.

You need someone else to do the manufacturing for you so hire someone to do it. That's as straightforward as it can get.

In chapter 1, I talk about choosing a product with "**High-Potential for Private Labelling as a Beginner**" as part of your criteria.

As a beginner seller, you are not likely to compete with big brands that have expensive products. So choosing a product that has a manufacturing cost of more than $100 per item is out of the way for now.

Imagine spending $100 an item and ordering 1,000 pieces of that product. That will cost you $100,000 just for the product itself.

So in the beginning, choose something that you can manufacture for $20 or less.

Another thing that you have to look at is the manufacturer's options.
Are there lots of manufacturers creating the type of product that you want to create?

If there are only 2 manufacturers in the world who can create the product that you want, then you'll have less option and that product is probably either mega expensive to produce or nobody wants it in the first place.

The third factor to look at is the brand building cost. How much do you need to spend to convince the customers to buy your product instead of the competition?

Imagine trying to sell them a new brand of smartphone… that would cost you billions to do.
Now imagine selling them some new brand of yoga matt. You don't need to convince them to buy your product as long as it has the features that they want. That's what I mean by brand building cost. The former is hard to sell as it requires you to have a mega-brand. The latter is much easier because of the nature of what it is.

The 4th one is what I call Value-Added Options. Can you realistically add some features that will add some benefits to the users?

I talked about this in detail in the chapter about Value Skewing so I don't need to explain this further.

The last factor to consider is the legality of your private label.

Make sure that you can legally private label that type of product.

Some items will have some patents that are legally off-limits for other manufacturers other than the owner of that patent.

Now, don't worry about this too much though. If dozens of manufacturers can private label a product for you, then it is likely that it is legal and no patents are being violated for that item.

In summary, you have to consider the following whenever you're choosing a product to private label:

#1 - Manufacturing Cost

Make sure that you can afford it and it won't get you into all kinds of debt.

#2 - Manufacturer Options

Make sure that there are lots of manufacturers who can make your product.

#3 - Brand Building Cost

Make sure that it doesn't cost an arm to convince the buyers to switch to your brand.

#4 - Value-Added Options

Make sure that you can add other features that will add value to the customers.

#5 - Can It Be Legally Private Labelled?

Forget about any monkey business, okay?

A QUICK NOTE ABOUT OVER-RESEARCHING:

— Avoid the Shiny Product Syndrome

The dreaded Shiny Product Syndrome is a play on the word Shiny Object Syndrome, a problem that is experienced by new and even pro-sellers alike.

Once you've chosen a product, I recommend that you stop searching for new items to sell for a while. Just focus all your energy on that product and make sure that you're sourcing a quality product.
I guarantee you that you will always find other products that are "better" than the one you already found. But putting your attention into dozens of products isn't going to do you any good.

If you focus on one (or two at max), you'll be able to quickly test if that product is worth scaling. SO FOCUS, FOCUS, FOCUS.

Bonus Chapter #3
- Profitability Calculator

For you to have a more streamlined process for calculating product profitability, I want to show you a simple free tool from Jungle Scout that's going to make life easier for you.

Take note that I did not create this tool and I'm only giving away the link because I found it quite helpful.

I use this profitability calculator to make sure that my margins are solid.

You can download the file here:

https://junglescout.grsm.io/fbacalculator

Conclusion

There you have it. A simple, beginner-friendly way of doing product research as a private label seller on Amazon.

I'm not going to lie. I've read other Amazon product research books before I started writing this one. Some of them are good and some of them are flat out wrong, in my opinion.

Although I appreciate the "keyword centric, numbers backed" way of trying to do product research – I'm not exactly sure if I would recommend using that as your sole research method. Most of the successful FBA sellers I know focus on value-building instead of just the Amazon search terms, keyword based type of product research.

I guess it all depends on what you want to achieve.

The research method I showed you in this book is for people who want to be in this business for the long-term. Those who aren't looking for a way to just make a quick buck. People who are committed to building a brand… someone committed to building something that they can be proud of.

The truth is there's a lot of stuff that you just have to figure out on your own. And that involves some trial and error – sometimes, even painful ones.

With that said, I wouldn't stop you from reading and applying research methods by other authors. I'm sure that you'll learn a lot of other techniques from those books.

However, I don't want you to rely on tools and software. I don't want you to become dependent of the tools that you have.

Imagine for a second that you are one of the 10,000 people who bought Mr. FBA Guru's course about AMAZON FBA.

Mr. FBA Guru teaches the software based kind of product research, so now, 10,000 people are doing the same thing and are probably even finding the same niche markets and same keywords. In this case, 200 out of the 10,000 people will probably order the same type of product in the same type of niches [and they will probably use the same supplier as well].

Imagine how terrible this would be for these people. They basically have no differentiation and their research was only based on the number of keywords they found for that product.

They didn't do any market analysis. They didn't do any research about what the market really needs. They didn't try to find problems and solutions. They just look at the data, chuck it in their excel files and start ordering that unproven product.

That's the danger of only relying on tools for your research. I'm not saying that they are useless, not at all. In fact, I actually use keyword and market research tools available in the market for my own business. The key here is to use them as a complimentary way of research instead of using them as your main research method.

Amazon FBA product research is my favorite part of the process because I always focus first on the fundamentals. Remember, no amount of data will ever guarantee a product's profitability. All you can do is to create value for your customers and they will decide whether it's worth paying for or not.

I wish you all the best in doing your product research!

Ciao,

Red

Review Request

As you might already know, reviews are the lifeblood of every author out there. If you found some value in this one, allow me to humbly ask for a review on Amazon as it does help in spreading my message.

https://www.amazon.com/gp/product/B084JRT8FN

Thank you so much and good luck with your e-commerce business.

Fulfillment by Amazon for Beginners

If you like to learn a simple and step by step way of getting started with Amazon FBA, I recommend that you check out my other book **AMAZON FBA Step by Step (by Red Mikhail).**

Just like this one, it has a very simple language and conversational tone to it. If you found this book valuable, then you will like that book as well.

OTHER BOOKS

I also have other books about making money online through different ways, check them out here:

Amazon's Associate Program

https://www.amazon.com/gp/product/B019EV4QA0/

One Hour Dropshipping System

https://www.amazon.com/gp/product/B014PU7S9Q

Amazon Product Listing Formula

https://www.amazon.com/gp/product/B0142ZWRC2

AMAZON FBA FUTURE UPDATES:

We're just scratching the surface. In the next 6-12 months, I'm going to launch a series of books about:

FBA Product Sourcing

FBA Advance Traffic & Marketing Strategies

Amazon Wholesaling

Amazon Retail Arbitrage

Amazon Dropshipping

And many more books related to Amazon FBA.

If you want to make sure that you get a notification when these books goes LIVE, just simply follow my Amazon author page here:

https://www.amazon.com/Red-Mikhail/e/B00X3KJ2TO/

(Click the follow button on that page to get instant updates from Amazon)

Made in United States
Orlando, FL
27 July 2022